EXIT STRATEGY

THE RIGHTLYND CYCLE

Rightlynd

Exit Strategy

Sender

Prowess

The Wolf at the End of the Block

Red Rex

Lottery Day

EXIT STRATEGY

⚞ A PLAY ⚟

IKE HOLTER

NORTHWESTERN UNIVERSITY PRESS

EVANSTON, ILLINOIS

Northwestern University Press
www.nupress.northwestern.edu

SPECIAL NOTE ON SONGS AND RECORDINGS
For performance of copyrighted songs, arrangements, or recordings mentioned in the play, the permission of the copyright owner(s) must be obtained. Other songs, arrangements, or recordings may be substituted provided permission from the copyright owner(s) of such songs, arrangements, or recordings is obtained; or songs, arrangements, or recordings in the public domain may be substituted.

ISBN 978-0-8101-3883-4 (paper)
ISBN 978-0-8101-3884-1 (e-book)

LIBRARY OF CONGRESS
CATALOGING-IN-PUBLICATION DATA

∞ The paper used in this publication meets the minimum requirements of the American National Standard for Information Sciences—Permanence of Paper for Printed Library Materials, ANSI Z39.48-1992.

CONTENTS

PRODUCTION HISTORY

Exit Strategy, by Ike Holter, received its world premiere on May 18, 2014, with Jackalope Theatre Company at the Broadway Armory in Chicago. The director and artistic director was Gus Menary, with set designs by John Holt, costumes by Delia Ridenour, lighting by Claire Sangster, and sound by Thomas Dixon. The dramaturg was Josh Altman. The cast of the Chicago production was as follows:

Ricky. . . . . Patrick Whalen
Pam. . . . . .Barbara Figgins
Arnold. . . . . HB Ward
Luce. . . . . Daniel Martinez
Sadie . . . . .Lucy Sandy
Jania . . . . Paloma Nozicka
Donnie . . . . Jerry MacKinnon

An East Coast premiere by the Philadelphia Theatre Company in a production by Primary Stages at the Suzanne Roberts Theatre, January 29 through February 28, 2016, was directed by Kip Fagan. *Exit Strategy* went on to open in New York City on April 12, 2016, in a production by Primary Stages at the Cherry Lane Theater. The artistic director was Andrew Leynse, and the director was Kip Fagan. Sets were designed by Andrew Boyce, costumes by Jessica Pabst, lighting by Thom Weaver, and sound by Daniel Perelstein. The New York cast (the same as in Philadelphia) was as follows:

Ricky. . . . . Ryan Spahn
Pam. . . . . Deirdre Madigan
Arnold. . . . . Michael Cullen
Luce. . . . . Rey Lucas
Sadie . . . . Aime Donna Kelly
Jania . . . . .Christina Nieves
Donnie . . . . Brandon J. Pierce

EXIT STRATEGY

CHARACTERS

Ricky. Assistant principal. Casually professional head-case with a mile-a-minute mouth.

Pam. Old-school educator without a second to spare. End. Of. Her. Rope.

Arnold. Former nice guy turned stone-cold teacher. Lost something.

Luce. Ex-frat boy turned math teacher. Everybody's right-hand man.

Sadie. Assertive educator. Positive foot forward. Till she trips.

Jania. The youngest teacher in the room. Survived the toughest stuff. Acts like it.

Donnie. Student. Spits out words like hand grenades and holds nothing back.

LOCATION

Somewhere in Chicago. A crumbling public school.

NOTE: A slash mark (/) in a character's speech means another character has already started their next line; it's an overlap, and both characters are speaking at the same time. An ellipsis (. . .) in lieu of speech indicates that the characters exchange something silent and necessary. Parenthetical speech means the character is speaking at a (low volume).

PROLOGUE

AUGUST 16, 6 P.M., ASSISTANT PRINCIPAL'S OFFICE

RICKY: So you know what's great / about—

PAM: Stop.
> Please. Stop. Just, just, just *don't*. OK? OK? I mean, you're already *so far ahead*, Vice, come on: Just Please Please Please. Stop. The. Bullshit.

RICKY AND PAM: . . .

RICKY: I was going to ask if you enjoyed the cake.

PAM: . . .

RICKY: The, the cake? . . . The, uh, the chocolate cake. It's big, it's in the lounge, it's really, really uh I mean *it's large*, very, very uh . . . so I was / just asking if—

PAM: What the fuck are you talking about?

RICKY: This afternoon, I went to the Jewel and I picked up the cake, the big cake—it's chocolate, it's in the lounge right now and it's got the logo on it: "Go Tigers," right, (Go Tigers), uhhhh . . .

I was just wondering if you enjoyed it, I was just wondering if you had a taste; 'cause *this*, you know, this-is-supposed-to-be-a-fun-little-get-together.

PAM: . . . Chocolate?

RICKY: Chocolate-chocolate, two different kinds, actually. Or maybe just double?

PAM: You picked it out?

RICKY: I (well) I actually designed it, / actually—

PAM: You picked it out—

RICKY: I *picked it out*, yes, / that's what I did—

PAM: So, you went all the way to Jewel, you grabbed a big cake, you put it right in the middle of the teachers' lounge for us to, what, exactly, to just munch on?

RICKY: Welllllll, / sure, I mean—

PAM: For us to just "dig in," huh, really just / "chow down" and what not, right?

RICKY: I mean, it's pretty good, and who / doesn't like chocolate, right?

PAM: Just sit around the table and stitch and bitch with the gym teachers and that stupid secretary with the fake tits and the idiot janitor—*you just went out* and got us a nice big cake so we can just hunker down on the dog days of summer and "have a fun little get together," is that it, Vice, is that your big goddamn idea?

RICKY: You can just call me Ricky—

PAM: I respect authority.

RICKY: OK, Pam, OK, see, OK, see *there's where you're wrong* there, see, uh, I'm not I'm not the authority and to be perfectly honest—

PAM: You saved me for last because out of all those sharks swimming over there *I'm* the one who scares you the most—that's perfectly honest, isn't it?

PAM AND RICKY: . . .

PAM: The cake's fine. I had a piece. Nice office.

RICKY: Ohmygod, uh, ohmygod, thank you, Pam, thank you very / much—

PAM: You're gay?

RICKY: Uh . . .

PAM: Figured as much. Nice office, like what you've done with the place . . .

RICKY: I actually don't discuss sexual politics in the workplace—

PAM: "Sexual politics": what, are you screwing a lobbyist or something?

RICKY: I mean my *personal life,* I mean my private life, I mean / my reality—

PAM: Jesus Christ this is boring, I don't care. When's the Band-Aid coming off?

RICKY: The—

PAM: Look, 'bout twenty-five years ago we had a dog, beautiful collie or something, nice-looking animal liked to chase squirrels and shit on the Sunday *Times,* family friend till the end, all that jazz, all that, anyway one summer it died, sad times in suck city "boo-hoo-hoo," so it bit the big one, right, but you know what I did? Well, I'll tell you what I did, Vice. See before my kid got home from baseball, I went and got ice cream, I went and got a cake, I went and planned ahead, so that when my kid came home I had enough distractions to take away the feeling of that Band-Aid ripping off when somebody finds out that a semi-truck turned Sparky into rat food.

RICKY: Jesus Christ—

PAM: He's not here, honey, it's just you and me now, kid, you and me, and you didn't bring me down here to chit-chat with the Vice without some Band-Aids coming off. Hit me.

RICKY: OK.

PAM: Hit me.

RICKY: OK! Pam. The, the negotiations didn't go as smoothly as we expected.

PAM: Negotiations? What negotiations?

RICKY: OK, OK, well, for the last—well, since forever, really, uh, the school board has been making an active case to the city about the necessity and the strength behind keeping Tumbldn open but / since the last meeting with—

PAM: Yeahyeahyeahyeah I know, I know. What I don't know is why you'd call a one-way conversation with the city *a negotiation.* That's just a really interesting turn of phrase right there, Mr. Vice, it's interesting. Sorry. English teacher. Had to point it out. Twenty-two years, hearing the crap that comes outta kids' mouths twenty-two, sorry, *twenty-three years,* and still, whenever I hear something that grits my gear I gotta say, "Let's look at that, let's examine that." I mean slang's one thing, sure, but *completely rearranging the English fucking language* so that you can lie, to me, well then I gotta say something—

RICKY: They're closing the school. The end of the year. Low test scores, unfavorable conditions. Lots of—lots, of lots, of lots of stuff. No way around it. Locks on the doors, day after the last day of school, it's done, it's set, it's structured, irreversible. It's over.

PAM: That's it?

RICKY: That's, that's, that's a lot, Pam. That's, that's a lot of information. So / I thought—

PAM: Let us down easy, let us down quick. I get it Vice, I get it—but that's it? No blood, no guts, just tears and chocolate cake, chocolate-chocolate cake. This is it?

RICKY: People have been in and out of this office, all night, in tears—

PAM: Was it Arnold? Did he cry? I bet he did, oh Arnold, Arnold's just a little bitch, / isn't he?

RICKY: I'm here to offer you guidance and support. This is new, this is large, this is a shock—

PAM: I'm a Chicago fucking teacher, nothing shocks me, you stupid prick—nothing-shocks-me. Forty percent of our seniors graduated last year, Vice. One could say that *I had a feeling*. There's a gang that operates out of that 7-Eleven on the corner, they knock into me when I'm picking up smokes, sure, *I had an inkling*. There are twenty computers. For three thousand kids. Leaks. Holes. Even the paint's trying to run away from this place, Vice, even the paint. Nobody's having a good time here.

RICKY: Well, you know what, we tried—

PAM: No, *we* tried, *we* fought, we struggled, and we struck. Vice, we did that, with picket lines and moms making signs and arm over arm over arm, we did all that, we tried with all that, but during all that way back, where the hell were you?

RICKY: We, we we we need to talk about next steps for you—

PAM: "Because you-you-you-you care?"

RICKY [*the first crack*]: Because I'm trying to but everybody told me not to not to *with you* because you're always going to act like a crazy old bitch, I'M TRYING . . . I'm sorry. I'm sorry. I, I, I,/ I, I—

PAM: That's the first honest thing you've told me all night, don't apologize for that . . . I have a contingency plan. Little while back? Before the neighborhood picked up, back when it was just brown and black, before Trader Joe's? I looked around at all this, just looked around at all this and I said, "You know what? Pam. You gotta get a second act." I've made peace with that. You, on the other hand. Vice Vice Vice. What the hell are you gonna do?

RICKY: . . .

PAM: Oh man. You never even thought about you, did you? Oh, / oh, oh man. Oh man.

RICKY: This is about the—this is about *the teachers* that that work in this school / so—

PAM: Which is closing—

RICKY: Which means—

PAM: Which means you're out of a job, what the hell's gonna happen to you kid? Oh man, *oh man*—you know computers?

RICKY: Uh. "Do I?" Yeah, yeah, sort of, / yeah, yeah, enough—

PAM: Know computers, word of advice, that's all they want, that's all they care about. You good on phones?

RICKY: I mean sure, / why not, Pam—

PAM: There's a call center? Over north (write this down), call center called Industrial Excellence, tell 'em Pam sent you—

RICKY: Well OK, that's very nice of you, Pam, thank you very much—

PAM: No problem. How big's your dick?

RICKY: How big, sorry, WHAT?

PAM: Well, if the computer programming thing and the telemarketer thing don't work out, you can get some johnnys to jack you off on the big gay internet. *Come on, /* I'm trying to help you out here, come on—

RICKY: OK, OK, OK, I got it, GOT IT—

PAM: Jeepers.

[PAM *takes out a cigarette.*]

RICKY: Actually—

PAM: Actually what, you little prick? Actually what what—? My husband's dead my kids don't speak to me I live in a shitty little duplex two miles from this two bit blackhole and right now you're telling me I'm gonna spend the last thirty years of my life working for another shit-eating creep at another two-bit black hole so now what, what, what are you going to "actually" me about right here, right now—look me in the eye, Vice, what?

RICKY: Actually . . . a lady never lights her own cigarette.

[RICKY *pulls out a lighter, lights her smoke. Takes out one for himself, smokes.*]

RICKY AND PAM: . . .

PAM [*singing*]: *Tigers, hear us, Tigers, fear us.*
    Tigers, Tigers,
    we're true blue . . .
    Tigers, hear us, don't come near us,
    we are Tigers through and through—

RICKY: *We are Tigers, a-do-do-do . . .*

PAM: You don't even know the fucking / words, do you?

RICKY: I have no clue, no clue / at all actually—

PAM [*chanting*]: *Tigers, Tigers, mighty mighty Tigers! Stand together, moral fiber*—come on kid, pick it up / come on, that's the ticket, that's the ticket—

RICKY: *Stand together, moral fiber—*

PAM AND RICKY: *Tigers, hear us, don't come near us, we are Tigers through and through—*

PAM [*rapid fire, with scary determination*]: *'Cause Tigers do what Tigers do, we stand so tall the chosen few and through it all we never fall we waste 'em all with wherewithal don't make us stop we never do we never do we never do . . . Tigers, hear us, Tigers, fear us, Tigers, Tigers,* blahblah fuck it.

RICKY: You've been to a lot of pep rallies, I take it!

PAM: Imagine that—

RICKY: (I cannot), well there's gonna be more, before we're done, homecoming, coupl'a weeks, uh, spring fling, after that; we've still got the year, and don't worry about me, I've, I've got it covered, uh, I'm gonna apply for everything, or maybe go back to school, again, or or maybe put both of those together, so there we go. Yeah. There we go. That's a second act.

PAM: Mine's better.

RICKY AND PAM: . . .

RICKY: You're not half as scary as most of the people say you are.

PAM: I bet that took a lot of courage for you to say, / didn't it?

RICKY: I'm actually terrified right now, my heart is beating so fast, wooooo. Why. Um. Why do you hate this school so much, Pam? Just—just tell me. Let me—let me try to help.

PAM: I love this school more than I love myself—don't you ever, ever, ever think anything else. And I need you to know that, Vice. Ricky, Ricky, I need you to know that. I need you to know that, / I need you to know that, I need you to know that.

RICKY: All right, all right, yes, OK! OK. OK. You've just got a funny way of showing it.

PAM: Well. You don't have to like somebody to love them.

RICKY: Can I take a second and think about / that one please?

PAM: Take all the time in the world, all of it, just take it all, take it all. I . . . I don't have any more fucks to give.

[PAM *grabs her things to exit.*]

RICKY: Pam? You've been right next door, for three years—

PAM: Twenty-three.

RICKY: Well, three years for me—you've been right next door, and we never even said hi.

PAM: . . . Hi.

RICKY: Hi.

PAM AND RICKY: . . .

RICKY: Knock when you get in.

PAM: What?

RICKY: Just knock on the wall when you get in. I mean, come on, right, come on: Just so I know you made it back OK.

PAM: I'll knock.

RICKY: Such a long trip, right!

[PAM *exits.* RICKY *takes a second. We hear two knocks from next door.* RICKY *knocks back. Goes back to his papers ... In the next room, we hear a gunshot.*]

RICKY: ... Pam.

FALL

SEPTEMBER 3, 7:30 P.M., TEACHERS' LOUNGE

[ARNOLD *turns on the lights in the Teachers' Lounge. It looks like a piece of shit. Turns on the coffee maker. Goes back to the mailboard and takes down the* PAM MORSE *marker. Takes all of the papers inside of it, rips them up.*]

LUCE [*entering*]: Ohmygod, ohmygod, ohmygooooooooooood. The one time I try to be first, the-one-time I get here early—the only time I ever ever take a cab here just to be first on the ground and look at that, look who's here, Mafucking Arnold mafucking Reese, hahahaha, fucking Arnold Reese, how the hell are you man what up what up what up sir how you doing pound 'em out.

[LUCE *raises his hand for a fist-pound, expecting. He does not take it down.*]

ARNOLD: Hi, Luce.

LUCE: Don't leave me hanging, / man.

ARNOLD: Leave you / what?

LUCE: Hanging, here, I'm hanging right now don't leave / me hanging, man.

ARNOLD: What are you / doing?

LUCE: I'm giving you daps.

ARNOLD: You're giving / me what?

LUCE: That's all I want I'm just giving you daps giving you props / showing you love—

ARNOLD: OK, I want something too, Luce, / OK—

LUCE: Hit me man, / hit me.

ARNOLD: I want this meeting to go smoothly, and quickly, and correctly. I don't want any catching up, I don't want any side-talk, I don't want any questioning of my *intention*, any questioning of my *authority* . . . I don't want—and I cannot stress this enough—I don't want any, any, any one of *you people* to even think of asking me what I did with my summer!

LUCE: Why / not?

ARNOLD: Because it's a big fucking secret, so deal with it. Don't need it, don't have room for it: I want a little bit of respect, Luce. That's all I want.

LUCE: OK, wow. Wow wow wow, OK. Duly noted, totally, totally noted. [*Finally putting his hand down.*] Arnold?

ARNOLD: WHAT.

LUCE: I'm really, really sorry. About—

ARNOLD: Don't be sorry. Hey. "Gimme some daps."

LUCE: Uh, I think we may be kind of past that / now.

ARNOLD: No come on, I told you what I wanted, what you want is easy, come on: "Gimme some daps."

LUCE: You're really freaking me out, dude.

ARNOLD: Nothing to be scared of, I'm here to serve, happy to oblige.

LUCE [*hesitantly*]: OK. Check it out. This is some new-new-now stuff right here, so I'll just start it out slow—

[ARNOLD *knows exactly what this handshake is. They do an intense handshake that is equal parts Hood and Frat-House; it is LONG and it ends with a slow slide and instantly they exclaim together.*]

ARNOLD AND LUCE: "Pop it in. Pop it out. Pop it up. Let it shout."

ARNOLD [*starting to exit*]: So much fun we're having / already, look at that, look at that—

LUCE: Whoawhoawhoa / whoawhoawhoawhoa . . . Dude, how the hell did you learn that?

ARNOLD: I invented that, when did you catch on?

SADIE: Back at it one more time and here we go, / here we go: "Hi honey hi hi hi."

LUCE: Sadie! What up what up what up!

SADIE: Hi, how you doing Arnold?

ARNOLD: We start as soon as I get back, / no stop, no stops this time.

[*He's gone.*]

SADIE: Well hello to you too. (I can't even with him / right now I can't even.)

LUCE: How you doing girl? Looking good! Looking good with those Aldi bags, / OK!

SADIE: You hear about the mice? / You HEARD about the mice, you heard.

LUCE: Ohmygod, Sadie, the mice were like two months ago. The mice are gone, they got the exterminator / in here.

SADIE: No they didn't—

LUCE: Yeah they did / they told us—

SADIE: They wanted the exterminator but then the toilets busted over fourth of July and they got the plumber, there's no exterminator, so tonight I went out and I got this—

[SADIE *slams a tab of mousetraps on the table.*]

BOOM, guess who is BREAKING DOWN THE DRAMA NOW?!

LUCE: Uh, I would guess it's the same woman who puts rat poison in the same bag with FOOD FOR PEOPLE, / that's gross, Sadie, gross—

SADIE: Nonono, those fuckers gotta die, you know my friend Tina was / the one who found it, YOU KNOW—

LUCE: Yesssss, god Sadie YES we allllll / know about crazy paranoid Tina—

SADIE: Sitting in the caf, minding your own business, opening up some hot lunch and what you get, (what you get) "maybe some hot dogs maybe some nachos," oh no, surprise, YA GOT MOUSE SHIT IN YOUR NACHO DIP, / that's what you got, that's what's happening, not this time—

LUCE: I don't even eat nachos anymore after that, I mean . . .

SADIE: Whose coffee?

LUCE: Arnold's coffee.

SADIE: Don't drink that coffee, he'll hold it over your head, power-play-bullshit, don't touch it.

LUCE: Look, we're having a sit-down, grown-up-style, very professional adult meeting, Sadie, someone's got coffee, sorry, but I'm finna drink coffee.

SADIE: I got juice-boxes—

LUCE: OHMYGOD SHUT UP! / Yeah, yeah, yeah-yeah-yeah DAMN BOI.

SADIE: Uh-huh, grape, orange, cherry-berry-berry, there was a sale, save the rest for my new kids, they're gonna love the hell out of me, believe that!

LUCE: How many?

SADIE: Uh, all of them.

LUCE: You're shitting / me.

SADIE: I shit you not, they gave me all her old kids, all of them. Rude, just rude. Rude, just rude just: know what, nevermindnevermind (I can't even), nevermind. Luce, "ohmygod how was your summer?"

LUCE: Finally. Somebody asked me ohmygod finally, yes, finalllly! Thank you, / thank you thankyouthankyou.

SADIE: Ohmygod, what is happening here, / ohmygod.

LUCE: Sorry, that's just like—like my *favorite question* of all time, maybe, so, thankyousomuch, uh, well first of all I had a party, in my backyard, you know, for the solstice—

SADIE: OK!

LUCE: But then when we went to light all the candles, I swear to god *shit took a dark turn—*

[JANIA *busts in with two sets of keys, a backpack, a handbag, a purse, a cellphone, and a coffee.*]

JANIA: Three Lord, right outside, in my parking place. Three Lord Gang, music blaring, smoking weed, sitting on top of the car, looking at me funny—Three Lord Gang, people, Three Lord Gang, right outside, maybe had a knife, maybe had a gun, / we're all in trouble right now.

SADIE: Hi Jania, welcome back.

JANIA: "Welcome back," please, *they* never left, I had to park across the street in Shocktown so they won't steal my hubcaps.

LUCE: Your car doesn't have any hubcaps.

JANIA: Yeah, whatever, I'm talking about my bumper—

LUCE: Uh, when did you get a bump / er?

SADIE: How's that window doing, Jania, still got that Walgreens bag on / it?

LUCE: Girl's got flashlights for taillights.

SADIE: Still have to open the door when you get to an intersection and kick yourself in a new direction?

LUCE: Fred Flintstone looking mafucker—

SADIE: *Ohhhhhhhh.* Oh snap! Oh snap! Oh snap! / You stupid! You stupid!

JANIA: Don't hate on Benita.

LUCE: Jania, I'm sorry, I'm sorry, for real I'm sorry, but your Mazda scares me—

JANIA: Don't hate / on Benita.

LUCE: Benita has bullet holes for bumper stickers, / Benita is scary.

JANIA: Those are not bullet holes—

SADIE: Uh-huh then what are those tiny little bump things all up on Benita?

JANIA: I don't know, I got her at the police auction— / how should I know?

LUCE: Benita's got BULLET HOLES!

JANIA: *You've* got bullet holes, shut up shut up shut up, you've all got bullet holes, you're all bullet hole people, just shut up shut UP SHUT UP! I HATE IT HERE, GODDAMN IT, I HATE IT . . . It's fine. They're probably gone. Used to it now. Should be. Don't call the police, I'm used to it.

SADIE: Jania, / we—

JANIA: Oh I don't care. Sadie. Come on. I don't care. You guys don't call, you don't write, I invite everybody over and you don't come, you don't care, you don't. Whose coffee?

LUCE AND SADIE: Arnold's coffee.

JANIA: Uggggggh, you don't care, you don't, you don't care about anyone—

SADIE: Uh—

JANIA: Sure, "the kids, ohmygod, the kids, the kids." Yeah, Sadie, we all know you're all about the kids (look at this oooh more notebooks more pencils and juice boxes and cracker snacks and ohmygod is that rat poison?).

SADIE: I'm thinking ahead—

JANIA: We've got nine months, start thinking further than that.

SADIE: "Thank you, Jania."

JANIA: Yeah.

SADIE: "Thank you very much."

EVERYONE: . . .

JANIA: I'm just going to say this now / so we can just get on with our year, OK?

LUCE: OhmyGOD.

JANIA: Don't try to be their friend. No more time for that. So stop. Stop passing out student loan submissions. Maybe, uh, maybe start passing out job applications, / start thinking further ahead like that, maybe, *for once*, just maybe give it a try, *tell-them-the-truth*.

SADIE: *I am giving you* / *one more* opportunity, Jania, and after that opportunity to stay silent is *over*—

LUCE: OK guys, guys, just, just hold it down OK, just don't do this, just *hold it down*—

[ARNOLD *enters and slams the door behind him.*]

ARNOLD: Let's begin.

SADIE: Arnold's right, this shouldn't take all night, let's get it out, get it done, / and get home—

ARNOLD: Luce, you're here because you're the only one who knows how to work that / that that that—

LUCE: PowerPoint-processor-projection. I'm on that shit, / don't even worry 'bout it.

ARNOLD: Moving on, Jania—

JANIA: I'm translating, just speak whatever and I'll / follow-follow-follow—

ARNOLD: That's what I like to hear.

SADIE: And I'm there to keep the peace: I'll do the first announcement, get everybody down there, we're good—

LUCE: Lights, camera, Jay-Z blasting on the speakers, and go—

ARNOLD: "Thank you for coming, and happy first day of school, Tumbldn. We're going to keep this quick for you guys because you've got a lot on your plates already, we're going to settle this once and for all and then first period will begin promptly five minutes after we close. Now: Everything? Everything changes, right now. As of June of next year, all of us are out of this building. This is the last year for Tumbldn. On June 16, locks go on those doors and after that, / we are processing—

JANIA: *Gracias por venir y feliz primer dia de clases Tumbldn! Vamos a ser breves por que sabemos que tienen mucho que hacer hoy. Hablaremos de esto de una vez por todas y despues comenzara el primer periodo. Todo, / todo cambia ahora mismo—*

ARNOLD: I'm sorry, do I just / keep going though, I don't—

SADIE: (Uh-Oh. / *Mmm. Mmmm.*)

ARNOLD: Jania, I'm sorry, are you getting all of this, / because—

JANIA: Of course I'm getting all of this, Arnold, why, / "what's the problem"?

ARNOLD: No problem, nothing like that, I'm just used to the old way—

JANIA: No more *old way* anymore, Arnold, just this— / OK, we've been over this, *just-this—*

ARNOLD: I know, I know, I KNOW, but still (I don't know) you know I feel like I'm at the fucking United Nations or something / I mean no offense—

JANIA: He's *starting* with me, you see that, you see that he's START-ING WITH ME—

LUCE: *OHHHHHHH / HHHHHHH!*

ARNOLD: What I'm saying is that it's about *tone.*

JANIA: "I understand tone."

ARNOLD: Tone is very important—

JANIA: *Me cago en la madre que te parió.*

LUCE: (Girl!)

ARNOLD: Thank you . . . "Everybody: This is not your fault. OK? (It's not your fault,) this-school-works, and it doesn't work because of the funding, or the city, this school works because of the people inside of it. Just because your school is shutting down does not mean that you can give up." Please translate that.

[JANIA *translates . . .* RICKY *enters during this and quietly takes a seat. As soon as* JANIA *finishes translating*—]

JANIA: What's he doing here?

RICKY: Hey. Uh. Welcome, welcome back, guys. I'm, just. Just. Just here to watch. So. I'm watching.

EVERYONE: . . .

RICKY: I mean, if that's / OK with a a a a—

ARNOLD: Now we're going to get the security thing out of the way, what's the guy, / what's his name?

SADIE: Ryan from the office is doing it.

ARNOLD: Good, thank you. Now this is where I'm gonna need some—some kind of correspondence, some kind of, some kind of back and forth, with you, some kind of / response—

LUCE: Talking about feedbacks? Rewrites? / You need rewrites, man?

JANIA: I've got some rewrites, / I do, see if I'm actually just repeating everything—

SADIE: Now we doing rewrites, I've got some rewrites—

ARNOLD: *No.* I put something together, I wrote it, I worked on it, and I'm going to say it. You're going to tell me if I'm off-base or if I'm on point, that's it. Correspondence, that's it . . .
"Let's talk about Pam Morse.
Ms. Morse worked here for—
years and years and years and years, and:
Some of you knew her. Some of you took classes with her.
Some of you did not have that opportunity.
But all of you have been affected by what she did last month.
Now let me say that again:
What SHE did last month.
Nobody did this to her. She made a decision, however long ago.
She followed through with that decision.
. . . I was lucky enough to know Pam for—I was lucky enough to—"
Luce, Luce, I need a picture or something—

LUCE: Yeah, sure I can get that, I mean, do you want the one that they used on the—

ARNOLD: No. Come on and focus, Luce. / *No, I don't want that picture.*

LUCE: Cool, cool, we'll, I'll just get like a different / one, like—

ARNOLD: Just get a picture of the woman that hasn't been flashed around on every news channel, can you do that, can you just locate anything else / but that, please.

LUCE: First thing tomorrow. First thing.

ARNOLD: "She was a very special woman and we won't forget that. Now, besides that . . ." (Besides . . . besides all that.)
"This is business as usual: Come to class on time. Represent your school, even when you're outside of it. This is our last year. Let's make it count."
Now: Feedback. Give me feedback, please.

LUCE [*after a pause*]: It's good, man.

SADIE: It's good, Arnold. / Arnold? It's good.

LUCE: Exactly. You got it.

ARNOLD: I didn't know if . . . I don't know if I should say "Pam" or "Ms. Morse," 'cause Pam / always hated that—

SADIE: But it's how they know her, / Arnold. Arnold, it's how they know her, it's good—

LUCE: They know what's up, they know, they get it, man.

JANIA: "Arnold, why don't you send me a copy of it so that I may work on my tone."

ARNOLD: It's in your mailbox already.

JANIA: I was kidding.

ARNOLD: I wasn't.

JANIA: Just slow down at the beginning, I'll try to only stop you three times.

ARNOLD: Make sure you get / all of it.

JANIA: I'll get everything, I always get everything, / don't worry.

ARNOLD: Let's move on, Sadie.

SADIE: Oh—so just like that, we're / just jumping straight to the next—

ARNOLD: We're keeping this professional, yes, "just like that," now you wanted to bring something up, bring something up.

SADIE: Well—I just wanted to try this idea out, here, just with a few of us, right, but I've been talking to parents, talking to parents of kids in other schools, just—just talking about how we deal with— this, all of this. There's already the All Together meetings to stop the shut-downs—which I encourage everyone here to join me in on Thursday, everyone, please, OK? but I'd like something a little more grassroots, one with less parents, less adults, one that kind of puts the heat on the kids, so: I started this idea called the "Next Stop Forward" project—

ARNOLD: What is that?

SADIE: It's a basic, (Back to basics, actually), walk-through of the neighborhood—

LUCE: You mean walkout.

SADIE: It's about looking forward, see, it activates the kids, it shows them that this is all hands on deck. This school *can stay open*—

JANIA: *No it can't.* Look, I worked at Johnson. Johnson High, good old Johnson, remember that? We fought and we fought and we fought and the day after the last day of school the city came with red tape and bulldozers and they knocked down the library. "Good old Johnson," remember that? The books were still inside.

ARNOLD: Sadie . . .

SADIE: Arnold—

ARNOLD: At the end of the day I hear you. 'Bout twenty years back, me and Pam, we tried to do the same thing. School-wide walk-out, protesting god knows what, thought we could get the whole school marching through the streets, show people what we were made of. Only two hundred kids showed up. Maybe a dozen teachers. Stopped by the cops before we got to the end of the block, nobody listened, nobody cared, this is it.
And the kids deserve to know that.
Pam knew that.
She would have wanted us to close out this year with dignity, then just—just move on. OK?

SADIE: . . . OK.

LUCE: OK.

JANIA: Mmhmm.

ARNOLD: OK.

RICKY: Actually.

EVERYONE: . . .

RICKY: Actually I was . . . I was the last person that was able to speak to Pam. I heard her . . . I heard her last words and they've really . . . It's a very hard thing to, to, to shake . . . But I don't think we could possibly ever know, or should try to pretend like we could know, anything that she would have wanted for the final year of this school. It's. It's. I don't think it's that simple . . . I didn't mean to—I'm just, just listening, but—just listening.

EVERYONE: . . .

RICKY: Thank you for—thank you for the coffee, it's, it's very nice, thank you. So! So we're back in full swing, huh, guys, that's . . . How was your summer?

ARNOLD: Let's take a *quick break,* / how's that for you guys?

SADIE: Let's take a five—

JANIA: Fine by me.

LUCE: Wanna smoke?

RICKY: Uh.

ARNOLD: Ricky, hold back just a minute, just for / a minute—

RICKY: OK.

LUCE: I'll be waiting.

RICKY: "Sure."

LUCE: You need / a smoke I'm just saying—

SADIE: Five minutes.

JANIA: Five minutes.

ARNOLD: "And we're off."

[*Everyone but* RICKY *and* ARNOLD *exit.*]

RICKY: I thought—I saw the, the meeting, was happening, and I just—I know I'm not supposed to be here, but / this—

ARNOLD: Ricky Hubble, I am going to say this very simply because I would rather assume you have no idea what's happening than think that you possibly know anything of the enormity of our situation.

RICKY: Maybe. Maybe we could do this later. At. At a bar / or—

ARNOLD: I haven't had a drink since you were able to. You will never see me at a bar. You will see me, right / now—

RICKY: I think—

ARNOLD: We are closing. And you weren't there when we asked for help, and you played deaf when we told you our problems, and you sat and watched TV on full salary as we stood outside with signs and screamed. We struck for weeks, and we lost.

RICKY: I just want to / help—

ARNOLD: The time for that is over, so please . . . Please concentrate on your administration. Please watch our backs. Please do that. But if you ever, ever stoop down to *teach* us: I sincerely hope you do it outside the confines of this crumbling building so that I may properly articulate just what kind of a man you are.

RICKY: Is that a—

ARNOLD: Is that a what?

RICKY AND ARNOLD: . . .

RICKY: Arnold? Arnold, I'm sorry.

ARNOLD: Stay that way.

[ARNOLD *exits.* RICKY *finally breathes, terrified.*]

WINTER

DECEMBER 2, NOON, TEACHERS' LOUNGE

[JANIA *unpacks her lunch and microwaves it.* LUCE *stares at his phone.*]

LUCE: Oh, wow.

JANIA: See?!

LUCE: Wow, / wow, holy holy shit *wow*—

JANIA: I told you, I told you, see!

LUCE: So this is like, this is like—

JANIA: If you're asking me (and nobody's / ever asking me)—

LUCE: This is like *wow*—

JANIA: This-is-big, Luce, it's not just on your phone, it's everywhere, whenever anyone goes to our website, our SCHOOL WEBSITE, *they get this.* That kid fucked up and if he fights it, if he's a fool, if he's like a dumb cocky senioritis-infected fool, well I don't say this lightly and it's not up to me (it's never up to me), but if it were up to me then at the end of the day I'd say he's getting expelled.

LUCE: It's not up to you—

JANIA: Yeah, it's never up to me. It's up to Sadie, see, / and lemme just say a few things about Sadie—

LUCE: Don't say her name, she's gonna walk in on us totally talking shit about her, that's like a classic Sadie thing / to do.

JANIA: She is sooooooo full of sanctimonious shit I can't even stand her lately / I can't, I can't even—

LUCE: (Daaaaaaamn girl you don't even care, do you, you just / don't even *give a fuck, do you?*)

JANIA: She's just strutting around, she's just fixing the world, she's just walking around the halls like she's Oprah Winfrey's bastard broke-ass stepsister, / *I can't even*—

LUCE: WHOOOOOA you lay off Oprah, Jania, YOU STEP OFF.

JANIA: OK well, Oprah LEFT US and now that shit doesn't work here anymore, she's done with this city she got smart she flew the coop 'cause *she knows what's up*, no time for dreams, time to stay woke and you know that, and I know that, but these kids, they don't, so when someone tells them ('scuse me) when someone LIES to them and says, "Oh you're so special and you're great and everything's going to be just fine," when Sadie puts / that in their head—

LUCE: Uh, hold up: They are special. They are great. And they are gonna be fine.

JANIA: I didn't / mean—

LUCE: You didn't mean to say our kids are stupid and dumb and useless: it just came out like that, right? Just—just sounded like that. Right?

JANIA: You do what, Luce, what: five classes a day, one hundred and fifty kids maybe, full workload?

LUCE: This isn't / about—

JANIA: I do two hundred, all day, six classes, from Down syndrome to any spectrum of autism and a bunch of other crazy shit nobody's ever even heard of to the troubled kids who you guys can't deal with so they trickle down to me and—I fight for them I bring them up I go out of my way, everyday, to prove everybody else wrong, I do that, OK, I do that . . . And they are *special*. They are *great*. But they are *not* going to be fine.
Fine is for white kids and North Side kids and all the other kids who aren't our kids; our kids have to work and work three times as hard or else nobody's gonna think twice, end of story close the book that's what's happening.
Now: this kid was told not to start that website.
This kid started it anyway. This kid went against the school and did something he shouldn't've and if there are no ramifications for that, then ADR that scares the hell out of me, Luce, that that that freaks me out. ADR, it scares me . . . ADR.

LUCE: Stop saying that, *what is that?*

JANIA: ADR.

LUCE: What is that?

JANIA: It's All Due Respect. Oh my god, don't you read the graffiti?

LUCE: Uh well, OK then, ADR, whatever you keep putting in that microwave smells like melted-down orangutan, / ADR, Jania!

JANIA: Don't hate on my food, DON'T.

LUCE: ADR.

JANIA: Luce, OK, usually you're nice and you're smart and you take my side because you know that we're both—

LUCE: Latino.

JANIA: *Smart*, shithead.

LUCE: OK.

JANIA: We're both *smart*. And I know this isn't up to me—

LUCE: Yeah, I know it's up to Ricky.

JANIA: And he's an even bigger idiot than Oprah Winfrey. Now I'm
sorry, but I'm not living in a world where I believe that the crazy
revolution of one high and mighty senior can suddenly turn us
all into Freedom Writers who can Step It Up to the Streets and
teach all these Dangerous Minds Mr. Holland's Opus. ADR, I'm
not drinking that Kool-Aid: *The Clock.* Is ticking. It's December,
Luce. *December.* You started looking for something else for the
fall, any other schools at all? *Oh no*, don't answer that, *of course*
you haven't: Start now. Get your résumé, get your recommenda-
tions, get it all together and don't wait.
Take it from me, OK? There needs to be a separation. If not,
you're gonna get trapped.

[RICKY *enters.*]

RICKY: Well let's not worry about that! OK! Uh I'm here to help, here
to assist, here to "hear," and Sadie's bringing the student down
here, as we speak, so just just just trust that we will deal with the
entire situation and finish this before it gets started OK, so nobody
needs to get suspended we just need to sweep this under the rug—
nobody's getting trapped and we're fine, we're great, and Jesus
Christ what is that smell where's that smell, are the mice back,
what's up with that?

JANIA AND RICKY: . . .

JANIA: I'm onto you.

RICKY: Onto what now, hmm?

JANIA: Onto you. I'm onto you, I know what you're doing.

RICKY: Uh, great, me too, Jania, I'm doing my job.

JANIA: No, you're not.

RICKY: Then what am I doing?

JANIA: You're Phiffering.

RICKY: I'm what?

JANIA: You're Michelle Phiffering this school and I am onto your voodoo, / I get you, I GET YOU—

RICKY: OK. (I don't know if that's a compliment or an insult / sooooo . . .)

JANIA: Suspend him, if you don't want trouble, trouble from Arnold, trouble from CPS, trouble from me, you read that kid the rights and you do what you're supposed to do you do / your job!

RICKY: I—

JANIA: You're a facilitator, so facilitate, / don't create, facilitate.

LUCE: Jania, knock it off—

JANIA: Do-your-job and say it Ricky, say it right now, say it to my face, just tell me right now—

RICKY: He needs to be suspended.

JANIA: And you're gonna do / it.

RICKY: And I'm gonna do it.

JANIA: Damn, right now, get it done.

[JANIA *exits.*]

RICKY AND LUCE: . . .

LUCE: "Damn, right now, get it done."

RICKY: WHAT is that SMELL? / I mean, my god, am I right?!

LUCE: "You're gonna do it, damn right, / you're gonna do it!"

RICKY: I looked deep into her eyes and I saw nothing, / it's it's it's mortifying.

LUCE: Don't look into her eyes, she'll turn you into a stoner, / don't do it, stronger men have tried.

RICKY: "Look at me, I'm Jania and I'm a rage monster." / I mean JESUS. Is she gone, like gone gone—

LUCE: "Get it done, get it done." Oh, she's probably running off to her car to tape up her windshield wiper again, she's gone, it's fine. *Now*: When in the hell are we gonna do lunch?

RICKY: Lunch?

LUCE: Yeah, stupid, / lunch.

RICKY: Well, you just ate and I'm skipping that meal, / *sooooo* . . .

LUCE: In-the-FUTURE, / when—

RICKY: During the day *I'm busy*, you're busy, we can't just / "do lunch."

LUCE: I'll pay.

RICKY: Uh, not about that / so—

LUCE: Oh "not about that"—you're like overdrawn thirty bucks. "Not about that"—you stole my fucking Hot Pockets last night. / "Not about that," uh-huh.

RICKY: *Shhhhhhhhh*hut up!

LUCE: What, you did, *you / know* you did.

RICKY: Not so loud *not here.*

LUCE: OK so let's just talk about lunch, you, me, let's do it sometime soon, because everybody else has like a total blast doing lunch, / everybody loves it.

RICKY: Well "everybody else" has has has has *disposable income* and *obesity issues,* so, sure, Luce, if you wanna be like everybody else then go ahead—

LUCE: Well yeah maybe I do wanna be like everybody else because "everybody else" talks about their relationships and doesn't act like they're living in a fucking goddamn fucking goddamn fucking goddamn fucking *convent.*

RICKY: Rectory.

LUCE: What?

RICKY: Rectory. We wouldn't be in a convent, we'd be in a rectory. For we are—men.

LUCE [*with crystal-clear precision*]: You are such a dickhead.

RICKY: How / am I a dickhead?

LUCE: You are SUCH a dickhead *and you know it* / so we don't even have to talk about it—

RICKY: No, uh, explain it to me, how, how, uh because I like to remain professional? Because I like to keep my work separate? Because I don't want want want people treating us / like we're some kind of an—

LUCE: You don't want people treating us like we're some kind of an Actual Thing?

RICKY: Yeah! No. Yeah. NO. / Nononono, shitshitshit OK OK OK.

LUCE: Thin ice. Thin ice, you are on thin ice, "my friend."

RICKY: I, I, I, didn't mean that. I didn't, I didn't mean that we / weren't—

LUCE: An actual thing.

RICKY: I didn't mean that.

LUCE: So what you meant was—

RICKY: I don't know what I meant, I had two meetings today and broke up a fight and had to make the morning announcements because I had to fire the gym teacher and the gym teacher usually makes the morning announcements and now I'm supposed to suspend some kid and *I'm tired*, Luce, I'm so, so, so tired and and and I don't know what I meant so I'm sorry, OK, I'm . . . I just want to lay. On the couch. In in in a fetal position eating a big sandwich until I get sick I just wanna lay on the couch and watch *Studio 60 on the Sunset Strip*, I'm so so fucking tired.

LUCE: . . . You fired Becky?

RICKY: I didn't want to—

LUCE: I know.

RICKY: It wasn't my decision, / I just have to—

LUCE: Lemme hug you.

RICKY: No.

LUCE: Lemme hug you.

RICKY: Not here, not / now, you know, OK, you know—

LUCE: Ricky, shut up, lemme hold you, and shut up, I know.

[LUCE *embraces* RICKY. *For the first time, we see him relax.*]

RICKY AND LUCE: . . .

RICKY: You smell like weed.

LUCE: That's not me. That's the school.

RICKY: Really?

LUCE: Really really.

RICKY: Kind of weird.

LUCE: You like it.

RICKY: I'll take it.

LUCE: Yeah you'll take it, you don't have a backbone, of course / you'll take it—

RICKY: Uh, I have / a—

LUCE: No you don't. You don't. And if you do then fuck you for never showing it, so. . . . I'd just prefer to think that you don't.

RICKY: That's not a nice thing to say. To me. Not. Not a nice thing, to say to me right now, / so—

LUCE: Hey—It's fine. OK? I've got enough for the both of us. Don't worry about it. So, there you go.

[SADIE and DONNIE enter.]

And there / you go, Donnie!

SADIE: Take a seat.

DONNIE: I know what's up, / thank you. [To LUCE:] What up Luce!

SADIE: Just sit down and take a seat. / I don't care what you know, take a seat.

LUCE: You better act nice / with this one, you better mean it this time man!

DONNIE: I know, I know, OK, I know what's up!

LUCE: Want some fries?

DONNIE: Hell yeah / I want some fries.

SADIE: Luce, leave us, / please, Luce, leave us, come on come on come on—

LUCE [*exiting*]: Fine (Fine), nevermind, / you don't want 'em anyway, trust me, hey, BYE!

DONNIE: Keep in mind I haven't eaten / lunch yet, haven't eaten anything, soooo—

SADIE: (Luce, be gone), Look, I need to get back to class right after the bell so that's ten minutes to figure this out, / so can we act quickly, please, can we do that?

RICKY: Ten minutes, more than enough time, uh, so let's let's let's just start at the top, all right, "Hi, my name is Ricky Hubble / and I'm the—"

DONNIE: Tie Guy.

RICKY: Sorry what?

DONNIE: Tie Guy, you're Tie Guy, everybody calls you Tie Guy / 'cause you've (yeah!) 'cause you've always got the tie.

RICKY: WHAT, really, that's, (what!) well that's great, that's, you know I like to have an assort / ment of—

SADIE: Ricky!

RICKY: OK nevermind about that nevermind. So we've got a situation here, / yes, a situation with—

DONNIE: All right, first off from the top I want to let it be known that Ms. Wilson had no part in this, I acted on my account and everything I did I did on my own, I just want that clearly stated, this is all me.

RICKY: Well I had no doubt in my mind about that but OK, that, that's very nice of you—

SADIE: He's not trying to be nice, he's trying to take credit, he has no remorse about this, he's proud of it.

RICKY: OK, is that true?

DONNIE: Is what true?

RICKY: You broke into the school website and you rerouted it to a Kickstarter / homepage—

DONNIE: Indiegogo. *Kickstarter*, how old are you?

RICKY: I turn thirty tomorrow, thank you for reminding me!

SADIE: Ohmygod, why do you look so much older than me?

RICKY: Wow, everyone is just on fire today! OK! Donnie, this is, this is you, this is all you, you're taking credit for it and you have no remorse.

DONNIE: Is remorse different than regret?

RICKY: Oooh, good question . . . / actually, good point, you know?

DONNIE: See there's *layers here, man,* it's like gray area all over / the place—

SADIE: *Nuh-uh,* oh no, not this time, / focus . . .

RICKY: Sadie, I need to hear the full story.

SADIE: My student hacked into the school, for that there are ramifications. He's trying to lead the class, he's trying to do my job, he's uppity.

RICKY AND DONNIE: Whoaaaaa/aaaaa—

SADIE: Whoa *what*?

RICKY: Can you *say* that?

SADIE: I can say it, *you can't* / say it.

RICKY: OK, good, just checking.

DONNIE: My teacher just called me uppity, can someone call Nancy Grace / and get her up in here, please—

SADIE: Nononono, Nancy Grace isn't coming to save you, now I need to get to class and I'm sorry, Donnie, I'm sorry that I'm the only one here who is not dazzled and impressed and blown over by the fact that you think you can just control the school, lead the school, teach people—that's my job, / that is my job, let-me-do-it.

RICKY: Just, just, I'm just trying to be fair here, and honestly, uh, I'm a little surprised, / honestly—

SADIE: What's surprising about this, / what?

RICKY: *Wellll*, not too long ago, you had quite the radical idea yourself, remember the walkout, / and—

SADIE: A walkout isn't begging for money, / how is that the same?

RICKY: He seems like, you know, he seems like he wants to help—

SADIE: You know how this ends.

RICKY: Well that's, that's ominous.

SADIE: You know how this ends, I'm busy, I need help, and I need you, Ricky, I need you to do your job because at the end of / the day—

DONNIE: At the end of the day you're mad 'cause as down as you think you are all the kids still only wanna listen to me. And I'm the only one in this school who ain't falling for your Teacher of the Year candy-ass bullshit. Try as hard as you want, at the end of the day, you are no Pam Morse.

[*The bell rings.*]

SADIE: Ricky Hubble: you know what to do.

RICKY: I—

SADIE: You know what to do.

[*She's gone.*]

DONNIE: I'm getting a suspension. Sadie wants to send an example, through me. But she wants people to like her, so she's making you do it. That's what's up, right? 'Cause if that's the case—and I'm pretty perceptive about this stuff, all right, that looks like the case—if that's what's up then I'm gonna withhold my statement and accept the consequences just, just right off the bat, man. Just give it to me and don't play.
Be a man about it, you know, I can I can take it, so.
. . . What? You forget the right paperwork, I can wait, as long as / it takes.

RICKY: You don't get to talk to me like that.

DONNIE: Sorry.

RICKY: Stay that way.

DONNIE: Permission to speak freely?

RICKY: Permission granted.

DONNIE: All right, thank you for that, look ADR I'm a senior I'm in like thirty-nine different places right now mentally, I'm like fucked up in the mind right now, mentally, and I'm not supposed to care but, WOW, *I do one thing* to show that I do and then I end up here. Look, I wanna raise five thousand dollars so we can get some new supplies, two of those three-hundred-dollar computers from the head-house, toilet paper, man, STUFF, I'm trying to help—

RICKY: Join the club, ohmygod, *we're on the same side,* I mean what do you think I do all day, honestly, man to man, what do you think I do?

DONNIE: I think you sit around in here telling people what they want to hear so you don't ever have to listen to the voice inside your head telling you what you actually need to do.
So then you probably go home.
So then you probably feel really frustrated.
So then you probably eat like a foot-long Subway sandwich and lay down on your couch like a little bitch and watch some stupid shit, I don't know, man, I don't know . . . I'm not trying / to like, you know—

RICKY: It's fine, it's fine, Donnie, just—just gimme *something.*

DONNIE: You need to save the school.

RICKY: Give-me-something-*smaller.*

DONNIE: That's it. My friend at Marshfield—Marshfield was supposed to close last year, bad building, bad neighborhood, low test scores all that, same shit—they fought, they won *they WON,* man, *here,* we're just / sitting back just—

RICKY: If you want to help, there's a meeting with the alderman this weekend.

DONNIE: Nobody takes her seriously.

RICKY: Well, I can find common ground with her on that front . . .

DONNIE: !?!?!?!?! *Then do something!* Fuck! Do something! Look you're not—dependent on the teachers at all, you're their boss, right, that's basically / how it works, right?

RICKY: It's very complicated.

DONNIE: You work at a public school, man, your shit is simple as fuck. Look, the way I see it—Ricky—

RICKY: Mr. Hubble.

DONNIE: Way I see it, if your job isn't the teachers or the students, if your job is the school, then I say you're failing your job . . . ADR.

RICKY: Let's move on.

DONNIE: But you did though, / right?

RICKY: The last time something like this / happened at the school—

DONNIE: You did, and now you're just sitting here, / just sitting here and watching it all just fall down.

RICKY: We suspended the student for three days and then instituted a detention / period of two weeks—

DONNIE: Your job is to protect this place, you-have-failed.

RICKY: Your job is to go to class and not fuck anything up—you failed at your job, so there's repercussions. This, right here, right now, this is my job, I'm doing my job.

DONNIE: Man, why do you hate this school so much? Look, I'll write down everything I did and sign my name on it. I don't care. Ms. Morse told me never to be afraid of the good that you do because sooner or later people are gonna come around and see that you were right: if it was really good, what you were trying to do, people always come around and they see that.

RICKY: OK. Donnie. I get it. Uh you you you lost someone very important to you. And that's awful. That's—so, uh, so you know what, I'm not going to suspend you. No. Week of detention. Nobody got hurt. And we need you here, so: All you have to do is say you're sorry.

DONNIE: Sorry for what?

RICKY: Sorry for putting that, that stuff online, just say you're sorry. We can work from that.

DONNIE: Look, I will never stop trying to save this place until they put the locks on those doors and kick us on the curb, I won't stop— But no matter what I do next? Won't mean shit. 'Cause I begged. 'Cause I said I was sorry. 'Cause I let myself be bought—

RICKY: That's a little dramatic.

DONNIE: Yeah, go fuck yourself man.

RICKY: . . .

DONNIE: Go fuck yourself. I don't care, you want an excuse, to get me outta here, 'cause you can't do it on your own, go fuck yourself man go on and do it.
Come on.
Come on comeonecomeoncomeon what are you waiting for man WHAT.
I'm giving you everything right now man, trying to make your job easier, what. WHAT.
The one person? The one person who got me? She's gone now, so I'm left with, what, Mrs. Wilson? Sadie? Sadie hates me, which I'm fine with 'cause at least she feels something for me, like, you guys expect us to just buck up and move on, well guess what, man, I'm not making seventy thousand bucks a year. I'm not teaching people outta the same books my parents used. I'm not bitching about parking places, getting tenure. Every day, since I was in first grade till eighth, every day we had to go up to the teacher's desk and ask for toilet paper just so we could go to the bathroom and take a shit. School's so broke you gotta dole out toilet paper like it's currency, every day you had to watch the whole class *watch you* take a piece of toilet paper and go take a shit, now you try people telling you that you're worth three squares of toilet paper your whole life you try watching your friends get the lottery and go to some goddamn special school, *you try* going here not for seventy thousand bucks a year *you try going here for free* you try all that, you try *for once* to fight back,

you try all that, and then you come up to me, *you look me* in the eye and you try and tell me to apologize for doing something when everybody thinks you're less than that less than *even that*, shit, go fuck yourself goddamn dumbass stupid ass tie-wearing piece of shit, fuck you fuck you fuck you fuck you *fuck you man FUCK YOU.*

RICKY AND DONNIE: . . .

RICKY: Donnie Bryant, please take take this notebook and pencil. You've left me no choice, let's not waste any more time. I think this is very clear, uh, please write this down:
"Dear Sadie Wilson,
"Thank you for teaching me. I regret to say that I will no longer be a student in your class.
"I will no longer be a student in your class because I will be too busy fulfilling my language arts credit as creative associate to assistant principal Ricky Hubble, as well as facilitating a new website for the school. Hopefully, with the"—are you getting all of this?

DONNIE [*in near shock*]: Dude—

RICKY: No time for that, come on, you're on the clock already, / all right?

DONNIE: All right—

RICKY: OK. "Hopefully, with the actions that are about to take place here at Tumbldn, this website will outlast my relationship with the school when I graduate. There will be a next year here, and I, as a member of the newly formed totally awesome group called 'Team Winning,' am going to help make that happen. We're going to save this school, and you can thank me later. Sincerely yours, Donnie Bryant."

DONNIE: Just "sincerely."

RICKY: What?

DONNIE [*back at it*]: The "sincerely" is already implying yourself, "sincerely yours" is redundant—don't worry, I got you, we're good.

RICKY: Great.

DONNIE: Holy shit, man . . .

RICKY: Holy shit.

SPRING

MARCH 13, 9 P.M., TEACHERS' LOUNGE

[*Coffee is brewing.* SADIE *looks at her phone.*]

ARNOLD: He's *late.*

LUCE: This is totally gonna be a good thing, look, Team Winning is /
doing something—

ARNOLD: Stop Saying That.

LUCE: That's their name, I'm just saying their name, Arnold, just /
saying their name.

ARNOLD: I know what's going on here. I know exactly what's going
on. And I'll wait. I can wait.

[DONNIE *pokes his head in. He is nicely dressed and carries a
clipboard.*]

DONNIE: Evening everybody, thank you for coming, / Ricky has
just a—

SADIE: Whatareyoudoinginhere, whatareyoudoinginhere, you can't
be in here—

DONNIE: Yeah I can.

SADIE: Why?

DONNIE: Oh, I got a badge / now.

SADIE: Why you got a badge now?

DONNIE: 'Cause I've been deputized.

SADIE: Meaning?

DONNIE: A higher authority / has given me authorization—

SADIE: "Higher authority" (please) *mmmhmm* authorization, authorization to do what, Donnie, tell me that, what?

DONNIE: OK. That's all the questions we have time for. Ricky will be
with you shortly, bye now!

[DONNIE *disappears.*]

SADIE: I ain't having it. It is almost 9:30. On a Thursday. And we are
still at school. I ain't havin' it. I need to go home I need to rest
up I need to sleep but now, for the last twenty minutes I've been
waiting here for an administrator who has shown me nothing but
disrespect, while our school runs through fads, while I'm told to
google this and indie-ho-ho that, excuse me but no, NO, I don't
ho-ho for nobody but nobody, NO—I ain't havin it, I ain't snacking on it, I'm not about this—but still I'm here on a weeknight
with you guys and kids running the halls like deputy dipshit and
I'm tired and it's too late to be around this hood and I am hungry
and I've got kids left with my husband who don't know a goddamn thing about how to work my DVR. I ain't with it, I ain't
about it, I ain't snacking on it, I ain't havin' it—

JANIA: But you're still here.

SADIE: Other things I Ain't Having, Volume 2: / *The Reckoning.*

JANIA: Hey, no no no, I'm on your side: we're all still here. Because we're being bullied.

[EVERYONE *makes booing noises, etc.*]

JANIA: Hey hey hey! Bullying is still a thing, I get the email alerts, it's real.
Now. All the first-floor people, this might be new for you guys, but all the first-floor people, we like to talk—

EVERYONE: We know!

JANIA: *Okaaaaay* (ohmygod,) anyway, we like to talk and see what's up if you know what I'm saying. We think they're planning something.

LUCE: Who's planning / something?

JANIA: Team Winning / is planning something, I know it—

ARNOLD: Stop Saying That. It Is Not A Thing To Be Said. / Thank You.

JANIA: Ricky and Donnie have created this army, this kind of like underground army thing, and at first we all thought it would go away once Christmas break ended, but it has not gone away (excuse me and ADR to Arnold), but whatever we're here for— it's been happening for a long long time. Sadie I'm with you, OK, "I ain't havin it" either or what have you, but see I think—this is just me—but I / think we *need*—

SADIE: Hold up . . . Hold up.

[DONNIE *enters with a boom box playing "Gangsta's Paradise" by Coolio.* RICKY *enters behind him and passes out paper.* DONNIE *turns off the song.*]

RICKY: "Good Evening and hi how are ya, everyone, / and thank you for coming—"

JANIA: (Hahahahahaha. / Hahahahahahahaha.) Hahahahahahahahahahahahahahahah. HAHAHAHAHAHA . . . . HAHAHAHAHAHAHAHHA!

RICKY: "I hope everybody's excited and optimistic for the test tomorrow, / I hope this doesn't run too long, / and if we're all ready, I'd just like to jump in, so—"

SADIE: Oh my god. / Oh my god. Oh my god. Oh. My. God. . . . No, no. No. Ricky. Oh. My. God. No.

RICKY: "So now, / I have invited you to this—"

LUCE: Hey, let him—HEY. Let him finish, all right? What the hell, let-him-finish.

SADIE: *Email.*

RICKY: What?

SADIE: Email, Ricky, you're better at email—

LUCE: You're great at email.

JANIA: You're telling me this *could have been an email?*

ARNOLD: Can I say something?

RICKY: It's important to do it in person—

JANIA: No paper trail.

ARNOLD: I'd really like / to say something.

RICKY: It's not going to upset anybody, / but what I need is—is—

JANIA: Then let us go, and turn on your computer, and send us an email, or a memo, right Arnold, like in the old days—no music, no spectacular stuff, pull-yourself-together.

ARNOLD: OK, I'm just going to say something and if I'm even off just a little just the smallest bit please, somebody please correct me. Here's what's going on right now: Jania likes to hear herself talk, Luce can't wait to get out of here so he can fire up his bong, Donnie can never seem to find a belt, and Sadie ain't having it. Now Ricky Hubble: Ricky Hubble does not care about you, Ricky Hubble does not care about this school, Ricky Hubble cares about his student loans and what he's going to tell his Facebook friends when the school he was going to work at for forty years shuts down when he's just getting started, Ricky Hubble only cares about Ricky Hubble. Now through all this I'm sure you're asking: "What about Arnold? What's, what's gonna happen to good old Arnold? What about that guy? What about him?"
Well, don't worry about Arnold. Arnold has his coffee. Arnold has a good book waiting at home. Arnold has watched for years as you guys have made his entire generation realize that there is nobody coming to save us, because every time you guys try to do something, you screw up every single thing in every single way, ADR. Now it's all fun and games here, right, and that's cute, OK, that's all real cute and I'm glad you got it out of your system / but the fact—

RICKY: (Just shut the fuck up.)

ARNOLD: Sorry, / what?

RICKY: (I said *just shut the fuck up*, Arnold.) Shut the fuck up.

EVERYONE: . . .

JANIA: (Hahahahaha / hahahahahaha!) Hahahahahahaha!

SADIE: Ohmygod, / Ohmygod, Oh-my-fucking-god I can't even, oh-my-god.

LUCE: He doesn't mean that, / he doesn't mean that. I swear, I swear, Arnold: he doesn't mean that.

ARNOLD: If you just said what I think you—

RICKY [*from the belly of the beast*]: I said every one of you dick-eating motherfuckers needs to *SHUUUUUUUUT*
THE FUUUUUUUUUUUUUUUUIUUUUUUUUUUUUUCK
UUUUUUUUUUUUUUUUUUUUUUUP!

[*The longest pause in history.*]

EVERYONE: . . .

RICKY [*tearing up the note cards as he speaks*]: "Good evening, thank you for coming—" now, here's where I would ask how your day went, but that would just take up too much of your precious time, and my depleting patience—so let's just cut to the facts. I call the shots, the shots are called by me, in other words—
I AM THE SHOT CALLER UP IN THIS MAFUCKER.
. . . And nobody cares about you.
Not the city. Not the mayor. Nobody gives a fresh-fat-flying-fuck, that's why this place feels like it's closed when it's still open. Remember that, guys, remember how this place is STILL OPEN. Oh, no, no, you don't, do you, 'cause if you did, if you did maybe you'd give a damn—I see you, I see everything, the kids do too—and I don't know about you, but I am sick, I am sick, I-Am-SICK of accepting that as fact. *We wasted* six months whining and and, and, bitching and moaning and, "Oh, what happens next," "Oh, don't get trapped," well, *if it were up to you butt-chimneys* we'd all just jump in the garbage disposal till we're chopped up sliced up *if it were up to you butt-chimneys* we'd just lie down and take it take it take it—*ohmygod you butt-chimneys make me sick*—

DONNIE: This. Is. Awesome.

RICKY: Thank you Donnie I really appreciate that.

DONNIE: No problem, / man.

RICKY: And I fucked up too, OK. I've been ignoring and avoiding and watching this place fall apart. But now, there is an army of three thousand soldiers that enters this building single file every day, and starting tonight, starting right here, we are activating every last one of them. Now every time someone gets an A on their paper, put it online, Instagram, Twitter, hashtag "Save Tumbldn." Whenever a student acts up, acts out, do not suspend them—we send them to the gym for two days and have them write a testimonial to how much this school means to them, and we'll put it on the website, hashtag "My School Rocks," 'cause if we can't get seventy-five percent of these kids to get a goddamn diploma then we might as well shut down this school tomorrow, hashtag "Get these guys out of here because somebody gives a shit."

DONNIE: Too big to hashtag.

RICKY: "OMG FML / SMD ADR!"

DONNIE: That's what's up! / That's what's up! (Yes!)

RICKY: Now these aren't big ideas, these aren't new ideas. These are simple, tiny little battles that lead the way to our war:
On May 3, we are marching.
An idea taken from Sadie from our first meeting (thank you, Sadie, ADR on that idea).
See, we're not marching through this neighborhood: because nobody cares.
We're not marching to downtown, to the offices. No, nobody cares.
We're going north. To the schools that people like better than ours. Where the people are nicer. Where the streets are whiter. We are marching to Lincoln Fucking Park, because if there's one thing people don't like, it's a big happy mob of color coming right towards them; we don't stop until we make the news. We keep going until they catch up, to us, for once. Let's *let them* catch up

to us because I am sick of reacting to what they throw at us. What closing. What test. What firing, people, people that I have to fire, people that I have to destroy—

I am not . . . *we* are *not*. We are not their *instruments*, not their tools, not their props. We are people in this city, we are *people in this city*, goddamn it. And trust that we have got this handled, we've got it sandwiched, we've got it clenched like the fingers in the fist—now you don't have to trust me, but trust in this: we have might so we fight we save tomorrow and start tonight, now please everybody everybody everybody trust that WE HAVE GOT THIS.

EVERYONE: . . .

RICKY: Donnie, what's next, what'd I write down?

DONNIE: Wait for applause.

RICKY: Well, OK, all right then.

JANIA: We marched at Johnson, and / at Johnson when we did it—

RICKY: This. Is. Nothing. Like. Johnson. That was unprecedented and will never happen / again, CAN never happen again—

JANIA: Don't you talk over me, you are fucking *with my career right now*, you are fucking with it, you let me speak, you let me speak. They didn't think we'd have metal detectors like it's the airport to get into middle school, they didn't think we'd have police officers in class, they didn't *they didn't think* anyone would ever close fifty schools overnight—there is no precedent until there is precedent you *hear me?*

RICKY: I hear you—

JANIA: You hear me. There is no time. We think we got the leg up, we don't. There is no time, trust me . . . But we do this, we do this right. Better this time, all hands on deck this time, keep it quiet this time. Fuck sitting back, fuck waiting for the city to act, I know how to annoy the shit out of people with my mere presence, I went to Vassar motherfucker, / WE GOT THIS—

EVERYONE: Yeah!

SADIE: We / got this.

LUCE: We / got this.

DONNIE: *We got this shit, motherfucker—* / we on it! We on it! We on it! *Woo!*

LUCE: Jania. You and me. We're making the speech tomorrow.

JANIA: That's fine, / keep up.

RICKY: You two go write it up. Sadie, Donnie, come with me. Arnold—

ARNOLD: You're an administrator using your power to bully innocent teachers into violating union policy. Mr. Hubble. I don't stop you? I'm not doing my job.

RICKY: Last chance, / Arnold—

ARNOLD: Last chance for you to keep your job. *You-will-fail* and when you fall down you'll take every single person in this room with you, *every single one.* I will not allow it. I will not stand for it. I will bring you down with such speed it'll be a wonder if you can see straight when I stop. Now this, this right here this is the line, I am drawing the line: we don't cross it.

RICKY: Anybody who wants to stay with Arnold, you are free to do so. Anybody who wants to come with me: I promise, I guarantee, I swear to god down on my knee that we will win.

[*Everyone exits except for* ARNOLD *and* DONNIE, *who grabs the boom box, starts to leave, but stops at the door.*]

DONNIE: Can I apologize?

ARNOLD: I've got friends who would love to stop this thing before it even gets started. I make one call: one call, and that's it, it's over, so don't apologize to me, I'm doing my job.

DONNIE: I'm sorry for your loss.

ARNOLD: . . .

DONNIE: Pam told me once, she told me that—she said you guys were like a team. She told me that you guys started together and were gonna finish together.
But she lied.
Cause now she's gone, and you're still here.
And that must really really suck, so: I'm sorry, man.
I'm sorry for your loss.

ARNOLD AND DONNIE: . . .

ARNOLD: I've never had you in my class, have I?

DONNIE: No.

ARNOLD: No, no, didn't think so. Lemme teach you one thing Donnie, just one thing: You are not special. And no matter what anybody tells you, no matter how much potential they say you have, how much intelligence, no matter what they say: there's always that little voice telling you that they're wrong. So instead of walking around like you own the block, maybe, just maybe, you should start listening to that little voice and Just. Stop. Fighting. You will lose. You guys always lose.

DONNIE: "I'm sorry for your loss."

[DONNIE *exits* . . . ARNOLD *crosses to the phone. Contemplates. Picks it up* . . . *Sets it down.* PAM's *there.*]

ARNOLD AND PAM: . . .

PAM: Long time no see, you look like shit, stop staring.

ARNOLD: . . .

PAM: Who on earth were you going to call? At this hour? Hmm? . . .
    Nevermind. *Secrets*, Arnie: they're all we have.

ARNOLD: Pam—

PAM: We could waste time with who and what and why but I don't
    have time for that, not right now, not anymore.
    I'm here. Deal with it.
    Still on the wagon?

ARNOLD [*pause*]: Cold sober.

PAM: Look at you, look at you. Well, I'm glad you started eating
    again. Least you've still got that. Good for the supermarket, not
    good for you, but still.

ARNOLD: Had to do something.

PAM: Scrabble. Chess. Online gambling. Eating. Arnie, as a coping
    mechanism, eating?

ARNOLD: I was on a diet / for a while—

PAM: Being broke isn't a diet, it's an unhappy accident—

ARNOLD: Lost ten pounds in a month.

PAM: Big whoop.

ARNOLD: Fuck you.

PAM: Somebody has to.

ARNOLD: "Dumb old bitch."

PAM: "Fat bastard."

ARNOLD: "Shit Eater."

PAM: "Hobbit Dick."

ARNOLD: "Butt-Chimney."

PAM: Hahaha! Hahahahaa! / Hahahahaha!

ARNOLD: Good one, right? Good one! That's new.

PAM: That's new!

ARNOLD: Hot off the presses / with that one.

PAM: "Butt-Chimney," you know, I always thought—

ARNOLD: It'd get better—

PAM: The slang, I always thought it'd get better, / but it didn't, did it?

ARNOLD: Remember "salty"?

PAM: Yes, I remember "salty."

ARNOLD: "Looking all salty."

PAM: "Brush that salt off your shoulder—" / yes, I remember salty.

ARNOLD: And then it was gone! Then it was just gone, / poof!

PAM: And then they stopped saying it! / Just like that!

ARNOLD: In today, / gone tomorrow.

PAM: I liked *salty*—

ARNOLD: You felt empathy for it.

PAM: I made others feel it, I poured the salt, I was the salt machine!

ARNOLD: You were good at it.

PAM: *I was. Ohmygod.*

ARNOLD: You were.

PAM: "I was." . . . How are the troops?

ARNOLD: They want . . . to do . . . a walkout.

PAM: Just like old times.

ARNOLD: Can't be like old times anymore, old times don't work.

PAM: Well, we got pretty damn far—

ARNOLD: And we failed. Didn't work twenty years back, sure as hell won't work now, can't have thousands of kids just storming the streets, they've got a few more months, that's it, that's all, that's / that.

PAM: I know what you're doing. You want to call the city. One of your old friends. Stop whatever these kids are trying to do, stop them from fighting, I know.
Don't. Don't make them stop. They want to make the same mistakes we did, well it's their school now, it's their life now, so let them fight, fight with them. You can do two things Arnie, from where I see it. You can fight the monster. Or you can become it . . . Smile, shitface. I just gave you the best goddamn advice you've ever heard.

ARNOLD: It's easy for you now, isn't it? You get to stand in the sidelines. Give off some advice. Judge.

PAM: Arnie—

ARNOLD: You wanted to get out, so you did, but now: now you're still stuck here. Just like the rest of us. So if you wanna go so bad, then go, just go, what's stopping you?

PAM: . . . Is this how you want to remember me? "Pam's gone, so just fuck it all, just fuck it all." I did what I did, my choice, mine only. Now look at you. You miss one person, and now, now you're trying to take something from everyone, for what? Arnie. Whatever was felt. Whatever was wanted. Whatever / it was—

ARNOLD: It was never—

PAM: Whatever it was, it is gone. We had a chance and now it's gone so WHAT. *Arnold.* What the hell are you gonna do now?

ARNOLD AND PAM: . . .

ARNOLD: I really, really, really miss—

PAM: Don't. Don't say it. If you say it, I have to go.

ARNOLD: I know.

PAM: You know, wow. "You know." It's really worth that much to you? . . . All right then, big shot, go ahead, go ahead and say it.

ARNOLD: You look—

PAM: I look incredible, you look like shit. Don't beat around my bush, we've already covered this, just say it.

ARNOLD [*slowly*]: If there was a time. Maybe. Maybe a minute. Where I made it. Where I made it seem like I didn't care, or understand, or love you. If that ever happened, please: consider that my fault entirely.
I miss you.

PAM [*almost a smile*]: "And we're off."

[*Blackout.* PAM *is gone.* ARNOLD *stands, alone, phone in hand.*]

(BASICALLY) SUMMER

MAY 3, 10:15 P.M., TEACHERS' LOUNGE

[*Right after the protest.* DONNIE *is seated, watching the news on his phone.* JANIA *hovers over* DONNIE.]

DONNIE AND JANIA: . . .

JANIA: What is that, who's that, what's happening?

DONNIE: What— / Whatwhatwhat?

JANIA: That, what is that, that, is that us, it looks like the walkup— / what is that?

DONNIE: What, no, no I think it's an ad for H&M or something? / What?

JANIA: It's not us, / then, that's not us.

DONNIE: Not us, not yet, I mean they were there, / right, like—

JANIA: You saw them, / you saw them—

DONNIE: I know.

JANIA: Of course they were all there, check CBS. CBS knows what's happening, what are we watching / right now?

DONNIE: We're on FOX—

JANIA: "FOX." Fuck FOX, turn to CBS, come on get with it, chop chop: "FOX." / Please, *we taught you better than that!*

DONNIE: All right, all right, all right! . . . Commerical.

JANIA: "FOX," ha, "FOX" / "FOX please," "FOX."

SADIE [*entering*]: Buses just pulled up.

DONNIE: All of 'em?

SADIE: All of 'em, everybody's going to the gymatoruim, where's Luce?

JANIA: Setting up the projector.

DONNIE AND SADIE: And the speakers?

JANIA: YES, *and* the speakers, / of course he's setting up the speakers.

SADIE: Good on him, good, I talked to one of the camera people—

DONNIE: What'd they say?

SADIE: First of all, they love us.

DONNIE AND JANIA: YES! YES! See?! SEE THAT? / Of course they love us, come on, of course!

SADIE: They said it'll air tonight or nothing at all, slow news day, gotta be tonight—

DONNIE: "Slow news"?

SADIE: I'll take slow news over no news—anybody see anything / yet?

JANIA: No we didn't see it. *Boy wonder over here put it on FOX—*

SADIE: You put / it on FOX, Donnie, FOX? I thought *you were the chosen one*?!

JANIA: I know, right, I *can't even* / (I can't even)

DONNIE: Come on, hey, *I like a little variety*, OK? / Some unbiased opinion, hahaha, hey, OK! OK!

SADIE: Gimme that / gimme that gimme that right now gimme gimme gimme your phone gimme gimme—

JANIA: None of *that*, none of THAT nuh-uh nuh-uh. / "A little variety." *Please!* Please!

DONNIE: You guys are the worst, you know / that, *the worst*—

SADIE: How can you even use this thing, / ohmygod what is happening what, what?

JANIA: You just turned the channel, SADIE, / you just turned the channel, gimme that—

DONNIE [*dancing and singing*]: Sorry, no remote, "New tech new tech. / Uh-oh, uh-oh oh! *New tech new tech. Uh oh oh oh!*"

JANIA: What's he doing? / What's he dancing for, what's happening, what is that?

SADIE: Boy, stop dancing. Nuh-uh. Stop dancing boy ohmygod.

DONNIE: Oh, COME ON. Can't you guys like take a second? We did it! Big-ass walkup, now that's all anybody wants to talk about, who needs petition sheets *we shut down streets* mafucker! Ten. Thousand. People.

SADIE: Four Thousand People. / Actually.

DONNIE: Many thousand people, whatever. WE ROCKED. Victory? *Psssh*, we all ABOUT that, done with THAT, been there, done that, got the T-shirt, came on it, / "*New tech new tech. Uh oh oh OH!*"

SADIE: Get your ass home, / go, go, gogogogogogo, get your ass home, GO!

JANIA: This is STILL A SCHOOL, you can't talk like that, this is a motherfucking school / goddamnit, GO!

RICKY [*entering*]: What channel? Hello! What channel, we need a channel—

JANIA: Keep it on CBS, it's gonna / be on CBS—

SADIE: Camera guy I talked to was from ABC, someone text Luce, / make him put it on ABC.

DONNIE: Dude, I am REVVED UP!

RICKY: You did good work, you / should be revved up—

DONNIE: Did she sound OK, did she sound all right?

RICKY: Sadie sounded great!

DONNIE: She skipped the whole section about pre-enrollment.

RICKY: But she said check the website—

DONNIE: I don't know.

SADIE: I do, 'cause Sadie is right here, / hello, HELLO, how are you?

RICKY: Sadie, you did great. Donnie, tell her she did great— / (you did great!)

DONNIE: You've got some stuff to work on, but really good start.

SADIE: I got a standing ovation.

DONNIE: It's a march, nobody was even sitting!

SADIE: I did good—

DONNIE: You did good.

JANIA: We need a toast.

SADIE: I did GREAT and we need PIZZA. / Donnie, Donnie, you want some pizza, you want pizza? I'M BUYING / EVERYBODY PIZZA!

RICKY: Sadie, there's way too many / people in there for pizza come on really, REALLY?

JANIA: We deserve a toast!

LUCE: Ladies and gentlemen, we are LIVE on CBS. / In OMG HD big screen, thank you, thank you very much—

DONNIE AND SADIE AND RICKY: YESSSSSSSSSSSSS! / That's what's up! That's what's up! / Wooooooooooooo!

[JANIA *pulls out a bottle of champagne, uncorks it, BOOM.*]

EVERYONE [*exclaiming, variously*]: AAAAAAAaaaaah. / Ohmygod. / Whathefuck?!

JANIA: A TOAST!

SADIE: You bring enough for the rest of the class?

JANIA: Hell no, lock the door before they come, boy wonder, lock the door—

DONNIE: We need to record this.

RICKY AND SADIE AND LUCE AND JANIA: NO.

DONNIE: I meant the students being happy, out there, not the teachers drinking on the job in here, / damn.

RICKY: Good idea, go to the AV room, / get the good camera.

DONNIE: On it.

JANIA: What is he doing with those keys?

RICKY: I gave him the keys, this is war, he's our commanding officer, he's got the keys—

SADIE: I don't got keys.

RICKY: Uh, because you're the chief lieutenant, and you command the commanding officer, he carries your keys—

LUCE: I don't got keys.

RICKY: Well, because you're the secretary of defense and you defend the chief lieutenant who commands the / commanding / officer—

JANIA: I don't got keys.

RICKY: Because the last time you did, you left them in the bathroom of Big City Tap when you were barfing your brains / out, no keys for you!

[EVERYONE *laughs and freaks out.*]

JANIA: SHUT UP you bitches! / Shut up.

SADIE: Boy gimme those keys, I'm coming with, soon as the janitors see / you with keys—

EVERYONE: "CUSTODIANS."

SADIE [*exiting*]: "*Custodians,*" shut up, I meant what I said (damn, correcting me), gimme those keys, walk walk walk.

DONNIE [*exiting*]: Fiiiiiiiine—

JANIA [*handing* SADIE *a glass*]: Waitwaitwait, *salud!* Hey girl, HEY, HEY, "*Arriba, abajo, / afuera, adentro!*"

SADIE: "*Adentro!*"

[JANIA *downs the entire glass;* SADIE *takes a short sip.*]

Ohmygod Jania, it's champagne, not a shot.

JANIA: I believe in dreams.

SADIE: That's good stuff, Jania.

JANIA: Thank you for the compliment. (People like my booze!)

[SADIE *is gone.*]

RICKY: "Who knew!"

JANIA: No like, really, who knew?

LUCE: Gonna join the line-up, you coming?

RICKY: I'm I'm I'm I'm / I'm I'm I'm—

LUCE: Yeeeeeees.

RICKY: I'm drinking, / OK, *can I do that?*

JANIA: We're drinking, let him drink!

LUCE: Uh, thought we could walk down together.

RICKY: We can walk back together.

LUCE: "We can walk back together."

JANIA: I need him, thirty seconds, / just gimme thirty seconds then
we go—

RICKY: She needs me, did you actually / hear that?

LUCE: Thirty seconds, and fix your tie, OK, / you look like a cheap
lawyer in like a bad Grisham movie—

RICKY: Does it look bad, it's like a weird tie I'm trying? / Does it look
bad? Does it look bad? (It looks bad.)

LUCE: You look sweaty and gross and tired and unhappy and
optimistic and poor, you look poor as hell. Congratulations, you
look like a teacher.

RICKY: That's the nicest thing anyone's ever said to me.

LUCE: Shut up.

RICKY: No, I mean it. I really. I mean it.

LUCE AND RICKY: . . .

JANIA: Oh just fucking kiss him already.

LUCE: Actually, Jania, we have an extremely professional—

[RICKY *grabs him; they make out.*]

JANIA: Yeeeea! Yeeeea!

    . . . .

    OK, no! No! OK, stop it stop it ohmygod eww, / ewww, nononono, what's happening, no—

RICKY: You started it.

LUCE: You like to watch, / you're like into this stuff, Jania, "I'm onto you"—

JANIA: Go, go, Luce, go there, we'll meet you, gogogogo.

[LUCE *is gone.*]

RICKY: We've, we've uh uh uh. We've never, you know, in front of, like *in front of* / someone—

JANIA: Who fucking cares?

RICKY: OK!

JANIA: Don't move. I have something for you.

[JANIA *grabs her purse, which is huge. She digs around.*]

    So last night I was sitting around and I was nervous and I was feeling sick about today and I was bored and I thought about how much I used to just hate you.

RICKY: OK.

JANIA: And then I thought, "Know what, lately Ricky has just been killing it and he hasn't been making me like disgusted whenever I see him, and I think maybe like a long time ago he could have been a good person!"

RICKY: This is great.

JANIA: So I decided I wanted to do something nice for you, something that shows you I care, something to say thank you—

RICKY: Are you pulling out a knife or a gun or—

JANIA: Thank you.

[*She hands* RICKY *a card. He opens it.*]

It's a recipe.
It's called "Sudden Notice," and it's gonna change your life.

RICKY: This is, this, this is for people?

JANIA [*the most open we've seen*]: I mean it. Try it, sometime, when nobody else is around. All these things, separate, gross, but together: they make you focus and they make you work hard and my Dad worked hard until it killed him. Teacher for forty years, ate this every day, every single day, and—I don't know, I want you to have it. I don't know why, but just take it and make it and eat it and don't stop, don't ever stop.

RICKY: Jania, that's a—Jania, thank you / very—

JANIA: *Arriba, abajo, afuera, adentro.*

RICKY [*haltingly*]: *Arriba, / abajo, afuera, adentro.*

JANIA: *Abajo, afuera, adentro.*

RICKY: Translation?

JANIA: Cheers bitch.

RICKY: I'll take it.

[*They drink.* ARNOLD *enters.*]

JANIA: Missed you.

ARNOLD: The least I can do is show up for the job that I am paid for, Jania, so I did. I was watching from the window. Seemed to go well.

JANIA [*grabbing her purse and starting to exit*]: After we close up, we're jumping in Benita.

RICKY: Ohmygod no, / no, nonononononononono—

JANIA: Ohmygod yes, motherfuckin' TIGERS, *whoooo!*

[*She's gone.*]

ARNOLD: We have things to discuss—

RICKY: Great, let's discuss tomorrow. Right now, I'm on TV.

ARNOLD: Just let me say this once. Just let me say this quick.

[*We hear a huge roar of applause and elation from way, way down the hall.* RICKY *closes the door.*]

You did that. You did all that.

RICKY: It was a / group effort—

ARNOLD: You did all that, that was you. You organized a plan. You got the team and: it was successful, it was incredibly successful, Ricky, and you need to know that, see, for the first time in my career, I can look upon the administration of my school and say you did something right. You did what I couldn't do. You tried. You did a damn good try.

RICKY: Ohmygod. Are you—*ohmygod, Arnold,* are you saying I did a good job?

ARNOLD: I said you did a *good try*—

RICKY: OK, OK, close enough, hahaha, OK, close enough, uh—thank you. That, that means—

ARNOLD: Wanted to tell you in person.

RICKY: Thank you.

ARNOLD: On the day after the last day of school,
the city will come,
they will put up red tape,
and they will bulldoze this place to the ground.

RICKY [*after a pause*]: They—they don't—uh, they don't *do that.*

ARNOLD: Well, *they do that now,* Ricky. Not just closing up shop—this whole place from front door to back alley will be gone, wiped off the block, might be a parking lot, might be nothing but dirt, all they know: this place is worth more to the city knocked down than it ever was standing up. It's done. Found out last week. Wasn't supposed to tell anybody, and I'm sorry to be the bearer of the badness, but I thought you should know soon as possible. Soon as this was over. Soon as you could take it. Look, *you tried.* People saw that. Whole city saw that.

RICKY: Wasn't enough—

ARNOLD: You did all that you could.

RICKY: No. From *you.* "Arnold." It. Wasn't. Enough.

ARNOLD: Kid—I've fought since before you could walk. Goddamnit *I fought, I am tired.* Now I could have called a few of my old friends, from downtown, soon as I heard about what you were planning, almost did, too, almost stopped your march before it got started, but it's your school, your life, why fight that?

RICKY: No, nonono. You waited until the, uh, until the one moment until the, the, the one second where we could feel, *where I could feel good,* for once, where I could *be happy,* you waited till I was on TV and then you took that—from me—

ARNOLD: Oh, it's always about you, isn't it?

RICKY: No, I / didn't—

ARNOLD: It's not about the school, it's not about the kids, this whole thing has always, always been about you, Ricky.
Look, I told you before it hit the papers. I did my part. I did enough.
You let them have tonight. Let them feel good for tonight, OK, they deserve that.
They all deserve that.

RICKY: Arnold—
Arnold, I, I'm sorry.
I just have one more question, and, and then you can, you can go, and . . .
I'm sorry.

ARNOLD: All right.

RICKY: Just one more question: What would Pam say if she could see you now? . . . Would she tell you to just stand in the window and watch? Would she tell you to just let all these people have false hope? Would she want you to spend months and months bitching and whining because the only person who could put up with your shit would rather blow her fucking brains out than / spend the—

ARNOLD: *IT'S*
GOTTA
GO.
It's gotta go.
. . . And if you ever, ever think

of putting her name
in your fucking mouth again—

LUCE [*entering*]: Guys. GUYS.

EVERYONE: . . .

ARNOLD: It's. Gotta. Go.

[ARNOLD *exits.*]

LUCE [*to* RICKY]: How bad is it. How bad did we lose? . . . You wanna
talk? You wanna *smoke*? Wanna walk back, together, to the
train—let's go, let's go get a smoke let's walk, let's go to the train,
let's go to my house *I've got you,* OK, whatever you want, whatever you need, *I've got you,* but you need to trust me, all right,
you need to look at me you need to talk to me 'cause you are
scaring the hell out of me right now / and—

RICKY: DON'T touch me.
Justjustjustjust . . .
It's over.
It's all—
Just *don't.*
"It's Gotta Go."

LUCE: He woulda torn you apart. Stepped in at just the right second,
if I hadn't—"Thank you." That's all it takes, to make this OK, all
right, "thank you."

RICKY: . . .

LUCE: You can't even do that, can you? Can't even do that. "Should
probably get outta here before they turn out the lights."

EPILOGUE

JUNE 16, 8:25 A.M., ACROSS THE STREET FROM THE SCHOOL

[JANIA *stands with a bottle of champagne. We hear noises of the crowd. They drift away.* SADIE *approaches.* JANIA *and* SADIE *look off, beyond. They look at the school.*]

JANIA [*after a pause*]: Who's watching your kids?

SADIE: New place. Western.

JANIA: Western.

SADIE: You're starting early. Should keep that down. Cops. / Security.

JANIA [*slowly*]: We were never friends, were we?

SADIE [*after a pause*]: My fault. I should . . . I should have just /
tried a—

JANIA: I should. "I should have." I didn't. These things? They *happen,*
to me, apparently very often, *to me.* Once, twice now, third time's
the . . . "There needs to be a separation."

SADIE: I don't—

JANIA: Well, it's gonna happen to you. Again. *To you.* You're nice.
Don't.
Keep it for yourself.

SADIE AND JANIA: . . .

SADIE: Gimme a sip.

JANIA: A little for you means a little less for me.

SADIE: Hahaha. "OK girl, / OK."

JANIA: No really, this was six dollars at the Jewel, I'm not fucking
around, / all mine—

SADIE: All right then, OK.

JANIA: All right then, OK.

SADIE: "There needs to be a separation."

[RICKY *enters.*]

EVERYONE: . . .

JANIA: Where's your tie?

RICKY: No reason.

JANIA: You look good in a V-neck, you should wear more V-necks . . .
I mean it.

RICKY: I—

JANIA: Luce is seeing somebody else now. For like a month. Maybe a
month now. Right after. I met him. He's nice.

RICKY: . . .

JANIA: He's not bringing him. So you don't have to meet him . . .
Probably not ever.

RICKY: Thank you. Uh. We . . . it's / just—

JANIA: Did you bring it? The recipe. I left a message. Did you bring it?
   I need that back.

[RICKY *hands over an envelope to* JANIA. *She rips it up.*]

EVERYONE: . . .

JANIA: Don't take my spot.

[*She's gone.*]

RICKY AND SADIE: . . .

SADIE: I—

RICKY: We, we don't need to—

SADIE: OK, I, OK—

[SADIE *moves away, still visible but out of easy earshot.*]

RICKY: . . .

[DONNIE *enters.*]

DONNIE: What up man, / what up what up—

RICKY: "Hi, Donnie."

DONNIE: "Hi, Donnie," whatever man, what up what up, uh, can we
   hug, / I mean what is this?

RICKY: Let's shake, we're shaking here, / we're shaking here—

DONNIE: All right, *damn,* "we're shaking here."

[DONNIE AND RICKY *shake hands.*]

Been a couple weeks, right? [*Calling out:*] What up, Sadie?

[SADIE *gives a half wave. A small, forced smile. Near her breaking point.*]

Hello? How you doing, I said / hey, Sadie—

SADIE: (water)

DONNIE: What?

SADIE [*quickly exiting*]: (water. water.)

[*She's gone.*]

DONNIE [*after a pause*]: She never liked me, did she? Not really. Did she?

RICKY: You didn't have to *leave.*

DONNIE [*after another pause*]: You didn't have to give up.

RICKY: If you actually / think . . .

DONNIE: Don't wanna hear it. "I get it." Dunno. I just thought that anytime white people came in and tried to save some school, shit was supposed to actually work. My bad.

RICKY: If we would have tried *anything.* Anything else, Donnie, anything else. They threatened *my job,* / they—

DONNIE: Oh, *your job.* OK, your job. Right.

RICKY: You had two credits left. Two. That's it, that's it, two and you're done. That was it.

DONNIE: I'll make it up.

RICKY: When?

DONNIE: I'll make it / up—

RICKY: When, / Donnie?

DONNIE: This summer, fuck, this summer. I'll make / it up.

RICKY: Maybe get a GED or / something—

DONNIE: *Pssssh. Fuck that*, man.

RICKY: OK, so now what?

DONNIE: So I'll finish.

RICKY: How?

DONNIE: I'll just go back inside and I'll just make it up.

RICKY: Back inside what, Donnie . . . ?

DONNIE: Your next job? Your next thing? Wherever. Whatever it is. You're gonna need an assistant, gonna need a second in command, so *put me to work*, man. Take me with you.

RICKY: Donnie. Donnie, I used you. I . . . used you to get a response out of people. I used you to get sympathy. I stood behind you and I stood in your way and I used you. I'm sorry, but that's what happened and now look at you, so—I'm sorry. Go over there. With your friends. Go take it all in, one last time, all right?

DONNIE AND RICKY: . . .

DONNIE: What else are you gonna do, man? What else can you do? This is you, that, that place right across the street? That's you, that's all you have. I'm gonna bounce. That's how I roll, used to it. You? You hate Arnold 'cause you think he owes you something, he and Pam, you think those old motherfuckers owe you something; nobody don't owe you shit man, *you-owe-me. You owe us.* You *owe me*, man, you owe me.

Always were just some dumb fucking faggot, weren't you? Just a. Just a stupid fucking fag, always were.

RICKY [*after a pause*]: Let me just say that it was an honor getting to spend my year with you.

[ARNOLD *enters. He has a lawn chair. Sets it down. Sits.*]

ARNOLD: Gentlemen.

DONNIE AND RICKY: . . .

ARNOLD: "And we're off."

[JANIA AND LUCE *enter.* JANIA *carries two bottles of champagne.* LUCE *carries a big duffel bag.*]

JANIA: Arnold, don't sit on that. / You need to stand, you need to stand up—

LUCE: We need to be off the ground, one of the demolition people said we gotta stand up or else the debris's gonna hit us right in the eyes like a / big tsunami.

ARNOLD: I wore my glasses, / what more do you want from me?

JANIA: He wore his GLASSES, OK, oh OK, you wore your glasses, please. Here. Everybody, here, champagne.

[SADIE *returns.*]

You too. Everybody. Drink. The kid too, come on: *Abajo, afuera, adentro.*

ARNOLD: Me.

JANIA: Oh come on, Arnold, you don't / even—

ARNOLD: Me. Give it to me.

[ARNOLD *takes a big drink. Passes it back.*]

   OK. OK.

[*Without looking at him,* LUCE *sets the duffel bag in front of* RICKY. *They're a few steps away from the group.*]

LUCE: You never came over so, I threw out everything that couldn't / fit, so—

RICKY: K.

LUCE: Yeah so . . . so yeah, just take it. So. There you go.

RICKY: Good-bye.

LUCE: What?

RICKY: I / said—

[LUCE *and* RICKY *finally look at each other.*]

LUCE [*ignoring* RICKY, *crossing back to the group and pretending nothing is wrong*]: HEY you guys see the cameras over there, we got ABC, we got NBC, we got FOX. Donnie, / your favorite, FOX—

DONNIE: Man, whatever. Fuck FOX news—

LUCE: He's back! Look at that, / y'all—

JANIA: I need to go, I told the first-floor people I'd stand with them, / by the bushes.

ARNOLD: Just take a second, old times, OLD SCHOOL, come on. Just a second.

EVERYONE: . . .

[PAM *appears, joining the line, unseen.*]

ARNOLD: Nice day.

LUCE: Real nice.

RICKY: Yes it is.

SADIE: *Mmmmm.*

LUCE: OK. So. So here they come. OK . . . OK.

ARNOLD: Jesus. Jesus Christ.

DONNIE: Why are there so many of them?

SADIE: (Ohmygod.)

DONNIE: That's . . . that's— / fuck, four, five, six,

SADIE: Ohmygod.

DONNIE: Why are there so many dozers, *that doesn't even make sense,* why are there so many dozers? That's too / fucking many—

RICKY: That's how many they need.

DONNIE [*breaking down*]: Well, one or two, that's enough, I mean they'll pay for that, FOR THAT. I mean, this isn't, this isn't anything new for them, you know, I mean they've done this before and they're gonna do this again so they should already know how to do this, they should already have this down, they should HEY! Please, please, please. / TURN AROUND, there's TOO MANY, *just turn around just just just just turn, around . . .*

JANIA: Donnie . . . Donnie. Donnie, Donnie, DONNIE, DONNIE . . . You fight. And you fight. And you fight, and you fight, and you fight and you fight and you fight and you fight . . . *We don't* beg. We don't *beg.*

EVERYONE: . . .

RICKY: *Tigers, hear us, Tigers, fear us. Tigers, Tigers, we're true blue. Tigers, hear us, don't come near us, we are Tigers through and through* . . . Am I really the only one who knows the words to that song, / really, really?

JANIA AND SADIE AND LUCE AND ARNOLD [*variously*]: We don't know the song. No one knows the song. / No clue, no clue. / What IS that? / Oh please.

RICKY: One time. I'll lead us. All right, I'll lead us, I'll lead us, one time. All right?

EVERYONE: *Tigers, hear us, Tigers, fear us, Tigers, Tigers, we're true blue. Tigers hear us, don't come—*

[*Suddenly, the sound of collapse. The buildings topple. The dozers strike.* PAM *leaves. Everybody is feeling the same moment . . . And it's too much.* SADIE *exits, nearly running away. Then* ARNOLD. *Then* JANIA. LUCE *exits.* RICKY *exits.* DONNIE *is alone. Terrified, lost. He stares into the collapse.*]